I LOVE
AUTUMN
IN
VERMONT

By Tim Dailey

For my Mom and Dad, and everyone who loves Vermont.

Covered bridges, bright red barns,

antique wagons on the farms.

Horses and cows, goats and sheep, more hooves in the clover than feet on the street.

A fresh-picked apple, a satisfying crunch,
a squirt of cider as you munch.

Pumpkin, rhubarb, blueberry too, fresh baked pies for me and you.

Sap from a maple tree, nature's candy so fine, the smell from a sugar house is simply divine.

If your pancakes and waffles are lonely and bare, add warm maple syrup for a heavenly fare.

Leaves change their colors to orange, red and gold, painting the valleys so bright and so bold.

Chestnuts and maples, walnuts and oaks, thick trunks lifting branches losing their cloaks.

Trout flash their silver in fresh water lakes, fed by mountain streams with crystal clear wakes.

Final bows for the flowers before the first chill,

bales of hay dot the meadows and soft rolling hills.

Evening airs cool as the harvest moon roams, fire places ablaze, keeping warm hearth and home.

Chimneys send smoke trails into the dusk, the smell of burning wood, a hickory musk.

The wind whispers secrets, leaves fall to the ground, a gust and a rustle then nary a sound.

A fall day in Vermont is hard to resist,

a must-see experience for the bucket list.

Tim Dailey lives in Littleton, Colorado with his wife and three kids (Joey, Logan and Clara) and their cat, Boots. When not writing poetry about the things he loves, he works at Dailey Partners (www.daileypartners.com), an investment banking firm that assists fast-growing companies in venture capital fund raising and mergers and acquisitions. Tim's favorite hobbies include playing the violin, building snow sculptures, and continuing to add to the 'I Love…' series. Tim hopes that his poems, along with the photographs and illustrations, will offer a moment of joy to every reader. Finally, he wants to thank the talented photographers, illustrators and book designers that have made this series possible. For more books from the 'I Love…' series, please visit: www.timdaileypoems.com.